MOODS OF
HADRIAN'S WALL

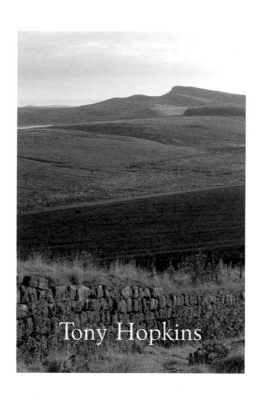

Tony Hopkins

HALSGROVE

First published in Great Britain in 2004

Title page photograph: *A September morning: east over the Wall from Hotbank towards Sewingshields Crags.*

British Library Cataloguing-in-Publication Data
A CIP record for this title is available from the British Library

ISBN 1 84114 368 5

HALSGROVE
Halsgrove House
Lower Moor Way
Tiverton, Devon EX16 6SS
Tel: 01884 243242
Fax: 01884 243325
email: sales@halsgrove.com
website: www.halsgrove.com

Printed and bound by Oriental Press

INTRODUCTION

Hadrian's Wall conjures a dramatic image of Britain divided by conflict and occupation, as Rome set the northern bounds to its empire. Stretched across the narrow neck of the country, the Wall weaves a thread of history into the fabric of the hills. In places the ruins are stark and inspiring, while in others they have mellowed into the landscape. Some stretches have been plundered for building stone so that nothing remains.

Two thousand years ago the Wall marked the boundary between the civilised world and the barbarians. For centuries the stones echoed to the bustling sounds of frontier life. Now they are silent and it is left to our imagination to recreate the story of the Romans in the North.

The Wall is now a World Heritage Site: a National Trail was recently opened beside it and thousands of visitors now explore its museums, visitor centres, forts, milecastles, temples and turrets.

Its setting could hardly be more varied. From east to west it stretches from the heart of industrial Tyneside, over meadows and moors and along the crest of the Whin Sill in Northumberland, then down to the rolling fields of Cumbria and the green lowlands of the Solway coast. A total distance of about 80 Roman miles, or 73 modern ones, with a continuation of milecastles and turrets down the Cumbrian coast and with supply bases at such places as South Shields and Corbridge.

This book presents the Wall in all its moods, as it is today. People who have walked the new Hadrian's Wall Path will recognise many of the locations, and for those yet to visit I hope the images will act as an incentive and an inspiration.

The selection of photographs and sites is subjective. However, most major locations are featured, and I have also included a couple of photographs of South Shields because it seems to me that the Wall was a coast-to-coast concept and benefits from the association. Where the Wall is missing from the landscape, where only ditches and banks remain and ghosts whisper in the wind, these pictures tell a story of a wilderness tamed and transformed, not by the Romans but by time.

Tony Hopkins

LOCATION MAP

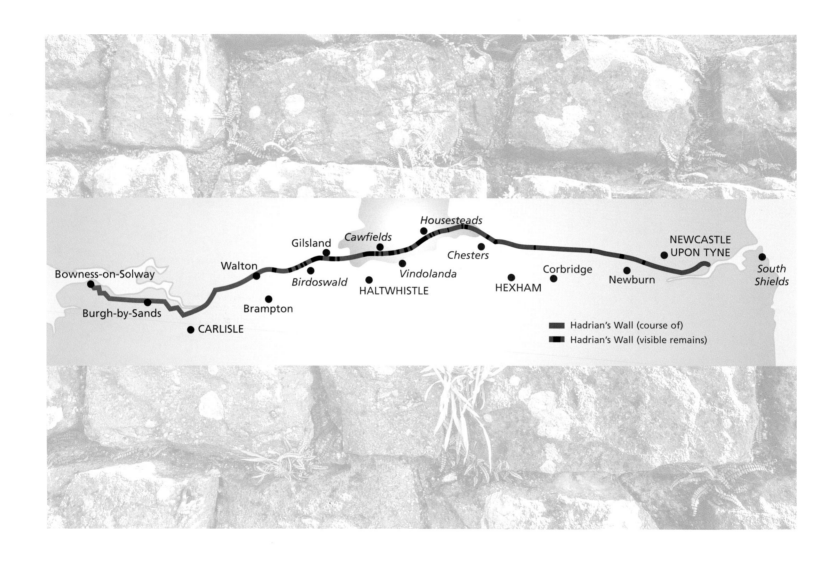

Bowness-on-Solway

Burgh-by-Sands

Walton

CARLISLE

Brampton

Gilsland

Birdoswald

Cawfields

HALTWHISTLE

Housesteads

Vindolanda

Chesters

HEXHAM

Corbridge

Newburn

NEWCASTLE UPON TYNE

South Shields

Hadrian's Wall (course of)
Hadrian's Wall (visible remains)

The face of the Wall: rumpled and crumbly,
turf-topped, lichen-covered – and looking its age.

The South Groyne light, at the entrance to the Tyne. Roman supply ships and traders would have nosed their way carefully into the river mouth here to dock at the jetty a few yards upstream. Maintaining the garrison of Hadrian's Wall was an essential and lucrative business.

The reconstructed west gateway at Arbeia Roman Fort at South Shields, overlooking the mouth of the Tyne. Arbeia was part of the Hadrian's Wall system, though it is several miles east of Wallsend. It was the main supply base for Severus's campaign of the early third century and housed most of the army's grain and gear. The reconstructed section of the gateway gives a spectacular impression of what the Wall must once have looked like.

Segedunum *Roman Fort at Wallsend, from the viewing tower of the new museum and visitor centre.*

The giant shipyard cranes of
Swan Hunter brood over the river and
make an impressive backdrop at the
start of the Hadrian's Wall Path.

Above: *The Black Gate, part of Newcastle's Norman castle, on the site of the Roman fort of* Pons Aelius.

Left: *Newcastle's Swing Bridge, in the foreground, marks the site of the Roman bridge at* Pons Aelius. *In the background, downstream, is the Tyne Bridge and the new Millennium Footbridge.*

One of the most extensive fragments of the Wall in Newcastle is at Denton, beside the busy A186. In the background is Denton Hall, built in the early seventeenth century.

Into the countryside, and an attractive section of Roman stonework at Heddon-on-the-Wall.

Dawn stubblefields, on the line of the Wall at Eppies Hill.

The Hadrian's Wall Path on a misty September morning, near Whitchester.

Looking north to Milk Hill, from the site of the Roman Fort at Halton Chesters.

For many miles the foundations of the Wall itself lie beneath the B6318, but the parallel earthworks are still an important landscape feature. A deep v-shaped ditch, covered in gorse here at Whittington Fell, runs immediately north of the Wall and was the first obstacle to any barbarian attack.

Ladder-stile along the Hadrian's Wall Path near Errington.

The B6318, called the Military Road (or Wade's Road) because it was built as a response to the threat of Jacobite rebellion, obscures a long stretch of the Wall's foundations. To the right (north) of the road here at Greenfield is the Roman 'fighting ditch,' while the dip in the barley field to the left marks the line of the vallum – an earthwork created to define the military zone.

Heavenfield, looking across the line of the Wall to St Oswald's Chapel and the site of the battle in which Northumbria's Christian King Oswald defeated Cadwallon the Celt and Penda of Mercia. The Wall, long-since dismantled for building stone, then stood at its full height and forced Cadwallon to attack Oswald up the steep north-west slope of the hill.

A short but well-preserved section of Wall at Planetrees. In the background is the valley of the North Tyne.

Above: *Summer pasture, with a stretch of Wall leading uphill to Brunton Turret.*

Right: *Mist over the North Tyne at Chollerford, upstream of the Roman bridge abutments.*

The Wall crossed the North Tyne via
Chesters Bridge, south of Chollerford.
The ruins of the Roman bridge
abutments incorporate a mill-race.

The bath-house (with alcoved changing room) of Chesters Fort on the west bank of the North Tyne. Viewed from the east bank, in the shade of a centurion oak.

A long straight run of Wall and ditch, near Tower Tye between Walwick and Black Carts.

Digging the Wall's ditch must have been hard work for Roman engineers. At Limestone Corner they had to cut through dolerite: after several efforts they gave up, leaving wedge-marks in the huge blocks. In the background, a walker follows the route of the Hadrian's Wall Path.

Big whin boulders at Limestone Corner.

Ragged robin and marsh thistle in flower, between the Wall and the vallum at Shield on the Wall.

Sycamore trees in a sheep-shelter on the line of the Wall and ditch, east of Sewingshields.

Sewingshields Crags: the Wall at last climbs to the crest of the Whin Sill, a volcanic intrusion with a gentle slope to the south and a steep scarp slope facing north. Looking east with Fozy Moss to the left.

Sewingshields Crags, looking west in evening sunshine. To the north, over a rolling ocean of moorgrass, is the southern edge of Wark Forest.

A drystone wall traces the line of its Hadrianic predecessor, along the crest of the Whin Sill from King's Wicket to Sewingshields.

Broomlee Lough: a pool of mercury in the leaden half-light of an autumn shower. The loughs of the Wall country are shallow glacial lakes, important for wintering wildfowl.

Midday, mid-winter freeze: Broomlee Lough looking east to Sewingshields. The footprints are those of a fox, probably hunting duck along the frozen shore.

Above: *The north gate of Housesteads Roman Fort. In the distance the Wall crosses the Knag Burn and rises eastwards to Kennel Crags.*

Left: *Housesteads Roman Fort: the most famous of the Wall forts, in one of the most dramatic settings. In the distance is Grindon Lough.*

Above: *Milecastle 37 and a well-preserved section of Wall, west of Housesteads. When built the Wall would have been three times this height, probably with parapets and possibly with its north side whitewashed to make it look even more intimidating to would-be attackers.*

Left: *August sunrise: sheep on the stonework of Milecastle 37, on Housesteads Crags.*

Milecastle 37, showing some of its internal walls. The rooms would have provided snug accommodation for the ten to twenty soldiers, who manned the gate and collected taxes.

The arched gateway through the Wall at Milecastle 37. Milecastles were positioned every Roman mile and their gates allowed troops to deploy north of the Wall when necessary. At other times the gates were used by traders.

Early autumn: fiery sunlight on the foggaged fescue-grass of Housesteads Crags.

A classic view east from Cuddy's Crags. Cheviot sheep follow the path down from Housesteads Crags.

From Hotbank over Rapishaw Gap to Cuddy's Crags. Walking the Wall Path along the switch-back of the Whin Sill can be more tiring than it looks on a map: for every steep climb to the crest there is an equal descent followed by another climb.

A few yards behind the Wall, running parallel with it and within the military zone defined by the Wall and vallum, the Romans created a Military Way or supply road, linking all the turrets and milecastles with the main forts.

Bradley Farm and the south-facing dip slope of the Whin Sill, rising in the background to Highshield Crags.

A mile north of the Wall: Hotbank on a very cold still day.

Five miles south of the Wall, near Staward Pele in the Allen Valley. The Whin Sill and Wall define the horizon.

The view south from the Whin Sill, over Grandy's Knowe, Crindledykes and Barcombe to Cross Fell and Great Dun Fell on the far horizon.

A half-buried section of the Wall at Highshield Crags.

A breezy summer evening: Crag Lough and Highshield Crags.

Above: *Frost in the shadows of Peel Crags. The vertical cliffs and columns of dolerite are the home of jackdaws and the hunting territory of peregrines.*

Right: *From Highshield to Winshields, over Steel Rigg and its secluded car park.*

The Long Stone on the crest of Barcombe Fell. The heather-covered ridge, a mile south of the Whin Sill, provides a fine viewpoint west and east. Vindolanda Roman Fort, clearly visible in the foreground on the west bank of the Chainley Burn, is one of the most interesting forts to visit and has produced some of the most spectacular archaeological finds.

Vindolanda Roman Fort, looking back to Barcombe Fell. The stone to build the Wall and its associated forts came not from the Whin Sill but from sandstone quarries at such places as Barcombe. An earlier Roman fort on the Vindolanda site was made of wood and was placed here to guard the Stanegate – Agricola's frontier road in the early days of the conquest.

Peel Crags from the bottom up.
Ferns and club-moss cling to the crevices.
The dolerite is volcanic and basic, but
not lime-rich. This encourages an unusual
plant community, with rock-rose growing
happily alongside heather.

Lichens cover most of the established south-facing stones of the Wall, turning it from brown to grey-green. Dry grass and yarrow stems top this five-foot high section, adding rich russet and gold to the textures. West over Steel Rigg, with Winshields in the distance.

A well-conserved and thoroughly-mortared section of the Wall at Sycamore Gap.

Sycamore Gap from the south. Nobody knows who planted the sycamore, but it became famous in the Kevin Costner film, Robin Hood, Prince of Thieves. *The same film located Hadrian's Wall somewhere between the White Cliffs of Dover and Sherwood Forest!*

The Hadrian's Wall Path crosses the footings of the Wall on the climb out of Sycamore Gap.

Some of the most impressive sections
of the Wall are those that plunge in and
out of sudden nicks in the ridge-crest.
This recently-conserved section is on
the east slope of Sycamore Gap.

Early winter at Castle Nick, looking east over Milecastle 39 towards Crag Lough.

Castle Nick from the east. The Whin Sill's 'nicks' are meltwater channels, created in the Ice Age when pressurised water, trapped beneath hundreds of feet of glacial ice, bored a way through the solid rock.

Rain driving eastwards over Steel Rigg. To the right, breaking the skyline of Hound Hill, are the tops of Walltown Crags.

Sunrise over Crag Lough and Hotbank, from Peel Gap.

Rainbow over Peel Gap: south-west to the Military Road, with the Twice Brewed Inn and Winshields Farm in the distance.

Heavy cloud and rain racing east to spoil the morning. From the road at Peel Gap, close to the Steel Rigg car park.

The climb west from Steel Rigg.
The wall here is not what it seems:
this is one of the sections dismantled in the
seventeenth or eighteenth century to provide
building stone for local farms. What survives
beside the obvious Roman ditch is a
field-wall, probably put together in the last
couple of centuries out of discarded rubble
from the Wall's original core.

Autumn sunshine on the Hadrian's Wall Path, west of Steel Rigg.

Half an hour after sunrise:
Barcombe, Morwood and the Tyne Valley
from the east ascent of Winshields.

For a few moments the whole world turns from apricot to peach, amber to vermilion. Close to the top of Winshields the Victorian field-wall gives way again to the original Roman Wall.

Swaledale sheep grazing among early autumn bracken.

Boulders on the windswept ridge of Winshields.

Above: *The end of the rainbow: a footpath from the high ridge of Winshields ('Whinshields', according to some OS maps) down to Winshields Farm, where there is a popular camp-site.*

Right: *The other end of the same rainbow, from the summit of Winshields Crags.*

Sunshine and showers at the triangulation column on Winshields Crags. This is the highest point on the Whin Sill at 345m/1132ft.

North from the shadows of Winshields: a dusting of snow towards Wark Forest, with the white-capped fells of Kielder and Deadwater in the far distance.

Footings at Caw Gap. The usual width of the Wall is about six feet: it was reduced from ten feet by the Romans after they had started work, presumably because they decided the original specification was unnecessary.

A low run of Wall, with Turret 41a in the middle distance, west of Caw Gap.

May at Thorny Doors: the Wall tucks into a shallow nick before rising again to Cawfields Crags.

A month later at Thorny Doors. In the background is Cawfields Farm and its silage fields.

East along the crest of Cawfields Crags. To the left is a steep slope of aspen and rowan bushes; to the right in the distance is Shield on the Wall and a very clear stretch of the vallum – a set of banks and ditches probably marking the extent of the Roman military zone.

Cawfields Crags: one of the best places for a bracing winter walk.

Rowan and willowherb, on the steep face of Cawfields Crags with Cawfields Farm in the background. Migrant thrushes, particularly redwings, strip the bushes of any berries by the end of September.

Cawfields Quarry is where, according to Collingwood Bruce's classic guidebook 'the visitor may form a clear idea of what can happen to the most august Roman monument… at the remorseless hand of industry.' Certainly an important section of the Wall has been lost, but at least the brutal slice through the Whin Sill allows us now to appreciate the geology of the volcanic intrusion – the columnar cooling of the molten rock to form dolerite.

Above: *Orchids and hawkmoths, finches and lizards, flourish in the quiet walled enclosure between the quarry face and the deep pond at Cawfields car park.*

Right: *A dramatic dawn moment as the sky turns crimson over Cawfields Crags.*

Crimson and gold ripples in the sky over Shield on the Wall Farm.

The sky cools and darkens,
a few minutes after the crimson dawn.
Looking east-south-east from Burnhead,
over Hole Gap and the Wall and vallum
to Shield on the Wall Farm.

89

A Roman altar-stone and the south gateway of Aesica Roman Fort, at Great Chesters.

Summer grazing on the dip slope of Cockmount Hill. The Wall is twenty yards to the right.

The soil is thin and the winds are fierce close to the ridge crest. These pines at Alloa Lea do not look very happy.

By contrast, hawthorn can cling to the exposed boulder-strewn face of the Whin Sill with obstinate ease.

Alloa Lea, east from the Nine Nicks an hour after a summer dawn.

Turret 44b, on the angle of the Wall as it descends to cross Walltown Nick. The turrets are numbered according to the milecastle they are closest to: there are two turrets between each pair of milecastles, hence the 'a' and 'b' notation.

Above: *Walltown Crags: the start of the best stretch of surviving Wall.*

Right: *Turret 54b on the crest of Walltown Crags. This turret was part of the earliest phase of wall-building and it probably functioned as a signal station. On the skyline to the south-west are the North Pennine fells of Geltsdale.*

The series of shallow clefts along the Walltown section of the Wall are known as the Nine Nicks of Thirlwall.
This is the fifth nick — those further west have been destroyed by quarrying.

Spring on Walltown Crags, looking west from a rocky brow on the north side of the Wall.

One of the best surviving sections of Hadrian's Wall, up to ten feet high, at Walltown Crags.
The north face of the slope, to the right, is covered in birch, aspen, hawthorn and rowan.

Courses of stone stepped into the east slope of the fifth nick on Walltown Crags. The facing-stones are dog-toothed and set into mortar.

The last ascent westwards along Walltown Crags. Beyond this brow an entire section of the Whin Sill was removed by quarrying in the early twentieth century.

Walltown Quarry. An attractive recreation site with access to the Wall (visible in the background, along the crest of the Whin Sill). The working quarry closed in the 1970s.

Thirlwall Castle, a medieval tower-house above the Tipalt Burn. Looking north from the line of the Wall near Greenhead. The gap of the Tipalt is where the barbarians may have attacked in the fourth century AD.

For centuries the derelict Wall was a perfect source for top-quality building material, so it is hardly surprising to find it missing now for hundreds of yards east or west of Thirlwall Castle. The mule sheep in the foreground have just come from market and are colour-rinsed.

Hummocks and ditches mark the route of the Roman Wall south of Gilsland, close to the Poltross Burn.

Milecastle 48, on the brow above the Poltross Burn. A few yards out of picture to the left is the Newcastle-Carlisle railway line.

The Irthing Valley in early autumn, close to The Hill. Beyond the river, the Wall crosses the pasture below Willowford Farm.

*One of the highest surviving sections of
the Wall, east of Willowford Farm.*

Oaks in early leaf, looking north across the Wall and the Irthing Valley.

A section of 'narrow gauge' Wall on a 'broad gauge' foundation. Hadrian or his friend Platorius Nepos, governor of the province, changed the specification half way through the building process.

Walkers on the Hadrian's Wall Path, heading east away from the Willowford bridge abutments.

The course of the Irthing has changed over the years: the abutments are now several yards short of the river bank.

An elegant new footbridge carries the Hadrian's Wall Path over the Irthing at Willowford.

Vandals. The authorities ask everyone to keep off the Wall.

Milecastle 49, Harrow's Scar, defending the west bank of the Irthing. Looking south with Cold Fell on the horizon.

*Close to the road, to the east of Birdoswald,
is this section of Wall, bearing a carefully-sculpted
phallus – a lucky charm to the Romans.*

Above: *Eastwards from Birdoswald; a long straight stretch of the Wall heading towards the Irthing and for Walltown Crags. On this side of the river, in what is now Cumbria, the Wall was first built in turf, because of a shortage of lime for mortar. The turf was replaced by stone after a few years. Here at Birdoswald the line of the Turf Wall, visible as a low grassy ridge, runs a few yards to the south to meet the fort at its east gate.*

Left: *Sunset over Midgeholme Moss, from Birdoswald.*

Above: *The east gate of Birdoswald Roman Fort.*

Right: *A loop of the Irthing, a few yards south of Birdoswald Roman Fort. The river has changed course and eroded its banks over the years, but it is tempting to think this view was enjoyed by the fort's garrison. Birdoswald must have been a more comfortable posting than* Brocolitia *or* Housesteads *on the windswept wastes to the east.*

Galloway cows, small but tough, on the line of the Wall near Wall Bowers.

The attractive red sandstone used in the Wall's construction west of Birdoswald has been scattered far and wide. A lot of the best stones ended up at Lanercost Priory. The facings of this field-wall and step-stile, next to the priory, look suspiciously familiar.

Lanercost Priory, built by Augustinian monks in the twelfth century and making extensive use of grey and red sandstone from the Wall.

Gravestone and wall of Brampton's Old Church, close to the Irthing. This building was also constructed of Roman stones.

East of Walton: a section of Wall recently entombed in earth to preserve the crumbling sandstone.

On the Hadrian's Wall Path at Swainsteads near Walton. In the distance the tall trees mark the site of the Roman Fort at Camboglanna / Castlesteads.

Hogweed in a hedge following the line of the Wall near Oldwall. Looking north into pastoral Cumbria: not everything north of the Wall was a wilderness even in Roman times.

Ripening barley and a downy birch, along the Hadrian's Wall Path between Oldwall and Bleatarn.

There is little visible stonework west of Banks but the route of the Wall is often obvious. Here at Bleatarn the Wall follows the grass ridge to the left while the vallum, topped now by a farmhouse, is on the right. In between is a pond, full of reedmace and brooklime.

A deep ditch near Wall Head. The tall hedge on the right marks the line of the Wall.

Carlisle's bridge over the River Eden is just round the bend from the site of the Roman crossing.
The wooded hilltop in the background marks the site of Stanwix Roman Fort.

Carlisle Castle, built by William Rufus in the 1090s and with a busy history in the Border Wars, dominates the river and road routes through the town. Nearby is the Tullie House Museum, which has an excellent visitor centre and contains the best Roman finds from the western half of the Wall.

The Eden at its most beautiful, looking upstream near Grinsdale. The Wall ran to the right, along what is now a wooded bank.

Beaumont: an attractive little hill, as the name suggests. The church has Norman origins and was built
on the line of the Wall, so it makes full use of handy Roman stones.

St Michael's Church at Burgh by Sands ('Burgh is pronounced 'Bruff'). A fascinating church with some bizarrely-sculpted stonework hidden inside: the village is on the site of the Aballava Roman Fort.

West of Burgh the line of the Wall follows the merse of the Solway. Nothing is now visible. At Port Carlisle a silted-up harbour marks an early nineteenth century attempt to link the coast with Carlisle via a canal and railway. The shifting Solway sands put paid to the venture.

Decaying oak breakers beside the silted channel of Port Carlisle.

Fog over the muddy Solway shore: a view east from Grey Havens to Port Carlisle.

A small Roman altar-stone (inscribed 'MATRI BVSSVIS') above the door of Hasket House (once the Steam Packet Hotel) at Port Carlisle.

Weathered sandstone altar above a walled-in barn door in Bowness.

Roman altar-stone built into a field-wall at the corner of the Kirkbride Road, Bowness-on-Solway.

East to Rampart Head: the Wall ended here, running down to the shore.

From Bowness west to Herdhill Scar. Dumfries lies across the Solway Firth.